THE LIFE AND WISDOM OF
HELENA
MOTHER OF CONSTANTINE

THE 'SAINTS ALIVE' SERIES

THE LIFE AND WISDOM OF

HELENA

MOTHER OF CONSTANTINE

Written and Compiled by
LAVINIA BYRNE

Hodder & Stoughton
LONDON   SYDNEY   AUCKLAND

British Library Cataloguing in Publication Data.
A record for this book is available from the British Library.

ISBN 0 340 70970 7

Typeset in Monotype Columbus by
Strathmore Publishing Services, London N7.

Printed and bound in Great Britain by
Mackays of Chatham PLC, Chatham, Kent.

Hodder and Stoughton Ltd,
A division of Hodder Headline PLC,
338 Euston Road, London NW1 3BH

CONTENTS

———◆———

INTRODUCTION

Who are the saints and why should we bother to know about their lives? We are inclined to think of them as heroic people who did extraordinary things, or as people who suffered a great deal and were somehow specially gifted or good. What we then forget is that, in general, saints are people like us. They struggled to know themselves better, to be more kind and loving, more self-accepting, less neurotic. They did not always succeed. They thought their attempts to live with integrity would make them closer to other people and to God. Often what they then discovered was that other people became harder to love and that God simply disappeared.

Yet they kept up the struggle. They believed that they were given one chance, that they had to live with a certain generosity, because this life is a preparation for the full glory of the next life. They then learnt that we are given many chances because all is grace, and the Christian life is a life of grace. So their schemes and plans for being holy were dismantled. All that was asked of them was a readiness to accept the gifts of God, including the final gift of heaven.

Saints come from every walk of life. They are men and women who share our concerns about money, power, politics, peace, energy, food, war, death, sex, love, privacy, the inner life, the outer life, harmony, balance. What makes them distinctive is that they looked beyond themselves to know how best to live and they discovered that God shared their concerns. If we read about them nowadays, we do so out of more than simple curiosity. Their lives are worth reading because we can learn from them. We look for more than a good example, though. The saints seem to know more than we do; they have access to a deeper level of wisdom than our own. They are gurus for our times. So when we read about them, we are quite right to seek an insight into the mind of God, who calls and inspires us all to the heroism of holiness, however we ourselves happen to live. Holiness is for all, not just the few; for a holy life is no more than a life lived in the presence of God.

In our materialistic and agnostic age, do the saints still matter? Have they any wisdom for us, or are they simply a pious irrelevance? Are their lives mere legends or do they have some significance beyond the bare bones of what history tells us about them?

Helena, the mother of the Emperor Constantine, stands at a turning point in history. For years the Roman Empire had struggled to get rid of the Christians. By the end of Constantine's reign, their religion had become respectable, their churches were everywhere, the Emperor himself had been baptised. What were the gains and what were the losses as the new religion emerged from the shadow of martyrdom? How could suffering and grief be interpreted in this new world?

Helena is an unlikely saint. We do not know much about her, but her name is linked so firmly to this question that it requires closer examination. What is a true cross? What is a false cross? How can we tell the difference? The life of Helena holds a key to answering these questions.

PART ONE

The Story of Her Early Years

'The tree of life my soul hath seen.'

PART ONE

———— ◆ ————

'The tree of life my soul hath seen.'

Legends and myths

When does a legend become a myth? Legends are old stories; they are suspect, because they cannot be proved. Myths too are old stories, but they hold human truth for us. No matter that they cannot be proved; the truth, the magic of a myth still works for us because it has inner meaning. It speaks to the preoccupations and needs of our own times.

One such myth is the story of Helena and her discovery of the true cross. The story is a simple one. Helena, the mother of the Emperor Constantine, was born in an outpost of the Roman Empire, at the city of Drepanum in Bithynia in Asia Minor, in the year 248. Later Drepanum would be renamed Helenopolis in honour of her. Little honour surrounded her birth. She was called 'a common woman not different from strumpets' by the church historian, Philostorgius. So she was an ordinary woman of ordinary stock. Later she would be the mother of an emperor, a divorcee, a pilgrim, a souvenir hunter, an unlikely candidate for canonisation, a saint.

The world into which Helena was born was similar to our own. It was a world of conflict and change, a world in which people were searching for meaning. That is why her quest for the true cross is about *now* as well as *then*, for the concerns of her world are the concerns of ours. New money, new opportunities, new ideas were everywhere. Who could offer a coherent view of how to live with them and use them to best effect? The old systems which had been used to govern the Roman Empire were worn out. An aristocracy of privilege had failed to deliver. The pagan gods too stood on trial. Even the military system with its proud Roman legions was in need of reform. Where was new life to come from?

There were civil servants, bureaucrats, army officers even, who had an inkling about the nature of this change. They had become Christians and believed that in Christ they had access to new life as well as to new ideas. Christ gave them new knowledge along with immortality, so they reckoned that they had an alternative way of living and of understanding their place within society. As one of the first of the great witnesses, Justin Martyr, wrote, 'You can perceive that the concealed power of God was in Christ the crucified, before whom demons, and all the principalities and powers of the earth, tremble.'

The concealed power of God was in Christ the crucified

The very earliest depiction we have of the crucified Christ is deeply shocking. It shows a crucified man with a donkey's head. His back is towards us, the head faces left towards a skinny little man with a crew-cut. The inscription reads, 'Alexamenos is worshipping his god'. The image was carved on the wall of a barrack's room on the Palatine Hill in Rome by soldiers who wished to mock Alexamenos. It reminds us that the crucifixion of Jesus was an object of shame and revulsion to those who were repelled by the Christian cult. But Christians themselves felt ambivalent about the cross, as we do today, for none of us likes suffering, and shameful suffering is the hardest of all to endure. For them, as for us, it had very little to do with any sense of the concealed power of God.

If anything the early Christians preferred not to remember that Jesus had been crucified. Their understanding of what it meant to be 'saved by Jesus' was mediated to them differently. They believed that the power of God was given to the world through the birth of Jesus. The very fact that the Word had become flesh was enough. The incarnation brought the creative and saving power of God into the world. Put simply, this means that they understood that when Jesus was born, we were saved.

In our own times a new theology offers the same kind of message. It tells us that we have for too long been dominated by the idea of original sin; what we need instead is a sense of original blessing, a sense of our own innocence. At first this theology seems to give us huge freedom. It says that we are not bad, that sin is not our worst problem, that we should be concerned to live in harmony and peace with each other and with creation. The only trouble is that we then discover that we are not as nice as we thought we were. Somehow we crave an explanation for sin and evil. So we return inexorably to the sheer fact of human sinfulness, to the truth of original sin and so to our need of redemption. We rediscover that we cannot save ourselves.

In the first centuries of the Church's history, the Christian community suffered terribly. The collective memory of Christians held scenes of indescribable anguish and these needed interpretation. A whole people suffers when individuals are persecuted. When the city of Rome burnt down mysteriously in AD 64, the Emperor Nero had sought a scapegoat. Christians became his target. Persecution was inevitable for a forbidden religion and Nero set about attacking them unmercifully. The irony is that the actual character of this religious persecution was dictated by the experience of Jesus. There are no artistic depictions of the cross from this time. It does not feature in wall or tomb paintings. Rather it was lived out in what happened to ordinary Christian people. This account is written in Tacitus' *Annals:*

All human efforts, all the lavish gifts of the emperor, and the propitiations of the gods, did not banish the sinister belief that the conflagration was the result of an order. Consequently, to get rid of the report, Nero fastened the guilt and inflicted the most exquisite tortures on a class hated for their abominations, called Christians by the populace. Christus, from whom the name had its origin, suffered the extreme penalty during the reign of Tiberius at the hands of one of our procurators, Pontius Pilatus, and a deadly superstition, thus checked for the moment, again broke out not only in Judaea, the first source of the evil, but also in the City, where all things hideous and shameful from every part of the world meet and become popular.

Accordingly, an arrest was first made of all who confessed; then, upon their information, an immense multitude was convicted, not so much of the crime of arson, as of hatred of the human race. Mockery of every sort was added to their deaths. Covered with the skins of beasts, they were torn by dogs and perished, or were nailed to crosses, or were doomed to the flames. These served to illuminate the night when daylight failed. Nero had thrown open his gardens for the spectacle, and was exhibiting a show in the circus, while he mingled with the people in the dress of a charioteer or drove about in a chariot. Hence, even for criminals who deserved extreme and exemplary punishment, there arose a feeling of compassion; for it was not, as it seemed, for the public good, but to glut one man's cruelty, that they were being destroyed.

The Roman Christians who were persecuted in the first century were not a lone group. Religious persecution dogged the steps of the early Church. It brought out huge courage in the individuals who suffered and their testimonies still carry weight. The blood of the martyrs was the seed of the Church. Justin Martyr's own story is a case in point. The final encounter with his persecutors is here described in the *Acts of the Early Martyrs*:

The prefect said to Justin: 'Listen, you that are said to be a learned man, and think that you are acquainted with true doctrine, if you shall be scourged and beheaded, are you persuaded that you will ascend to heaven?

Justin said: 'I hope to have His gifts if I endure these things. For I know that for all who so live there abides until the consummation of the whole world the free gift of God.'

The prefect Rusticus said: 'Do you then think that you will ascend to heaven, to receive certain rewards?'

Justin said: 'I do not think, I know and am fully persuaded.'

The prefect Rusticus said: 'Let us now come to the pressing matter in hand. Agree together and sacrifice with one accord to the gods.'

Justin said: 'No one who is rightly minded turns from true belief to false.'

The prefect Rusticus said: 'If you do not

obey, you shall be punished without mercy.'

Justin said: 'If we are punished for the sake of our Lord Jesus Christ we hope to be saved, for this shall be our salvation and confidence before the more terrible judgment-seat of our Lord and Saviour which shall judge the whole world.' So also said the other martyrs: 'Do what you will. For we are Christians and offer no sacrifice to idols.'

Rusticus the prefect gave sentence: 'Let those who will not sacrifice to the gods and yield to the command of the Emperor be scourged and led away to be beheaded in accordance with the laws.'

The holy martyrs went out glorifying God to the customary place and were beheaded, and fulfilled their testimony by the confession of their Saviour. And some of the faithful took their bodies by stealth and laid them in a convenient place, the grace of our Lord Jesus Christ working with them, to whom be glory for ever and ever. Amen.

When individuals or groups are terrorised, they

have little energy for developing any kind of philosophy or theology to explain why this is happening. Such rumination is a luxury. All they experience is the filth and the horror of what they live through. To record their experience accurately is all, for their principal concern is survival. Later generations would try to understand the sufferings of the early Church and make a connection with the sufferings borne by Jesus. Helena was to be an important link in the construction of this chain of meaning. That is why she is important to us too, because she reminds us that it is possible to knit chains of meaning and so to make links between incidents and events which at first seem random. For Helena, as the myth would have it, set out to discover the true cross.

Nowadays a search for the true cross seems less like a luxury and more like an irrelevance. This is because life appears so burdensome and we have become so accustomed to the fact of suffering that we do everything in our power to avoid thinking about it. We know about the cosmic scale of inter-racial, inter-tribal and

international conflict. We know about the every-
day agony of family or domestic suffering. God
is the first casualty of our sceptical age and a
suffering God is somehow an irrelevance. If we
think about God at all, it is to question or to
blame him. If we like religion at all, or are
attracted to spirituality, we generally choose the
nice bits, the bits that comfort and reassure us,
and the message of the cross cuts across the
wisdom of our age. Now this is a very good
reason for us too to conduct a search for a true
cross, one which speaks tellingly to our condition. But that requires a questing spirit and a
searching heart. How did Helena develop hers?

The soldier's wife

As a young woman Helena met up with
Constantius Chlorus. One biographer has called
him 'an obscure country gentleman from
Naissus'. They were married in 270. At that time,
Constantius' lowly origins did nothing to dis-
qualify him from preferment in the Roman
army. Many of his contemporaries came from
an equally lowly background. The Emperor

Diocletian was a freedman from Dalmatia; Galerius, his fellow Caesar, had been a cattleherd from the Carpathian mountains. This was a world in which talent would shine and find its own level.

When Helena and Constantius Chlorus met, Aurelian was Roman Emperor. The following year he had to build a fortified wall around the city of Rome because all was in turmoil. In forty-seven years there had been twenty-five emperors, of whom only one had died in his own bed. Reform was essential. At first it came with a reform of the army. The legions were disbanded and broken down into smaller, more mobile units. Cavalry were introduced. The total number of soldiers swelled to 600,000 with a huge infrastructure to take care of them all. This anonymous world provided jobs for Christians who became competent administrators and the architects of a new age.

Political reform was essential too. It came when the new Emperor, Diocletian, took office in 284. He divided the empire between the west, with Maximian as his Caesar in Rome, and the east where he took control from his court at Nicomedia. Things stabilised. A Christian middle class emerged, made up of business people and artisans who quietly went about their work and enjoyed the new prosperity. Theologians began to talk about God and the relationship of Jesus to the Father. They devised Creeds and set up Church Councils. There is a backdrop for this activity. For as Christianity spread, it did so in a climate of religious pluralism. The official state religion of the Empire was under threat from a number of sources. Syncretistic and cultic movements began to spread as people sought for meaning. They created their own beliefs and rituals because they found official worship inadequate. This was a hotchpotch world, where trade routes served to carry ideas and religious practices, just as nowadays the Internet carries random beliefs and messages. Orthodoxy breaks down as it has no way of controlling what people think and how they communicate with each other. This was a new age, so it produced New Age religions. Pagan orthodoxy was under threat. This meant that Christianity had a unique opportunity to 'break through' and offer a new religious dream. But equally, Christianity itself would be attacked from within with the birth of gnosticism, an unorthodox attempt to short-circuit access to knowledge about God from within its ranks. Helena knew about this syncretism because her husband, Constantius Chlorus, was attracted to the cult of Mithras. She inhabited a religious melting pot.

In 289, Constantius was promoted. He became the Caesar of the western empire. But with promotion came a new lifestyle and a new wife. Helena was unceremoniously given the heave-ho. Her usefulness was over. Constantius married Theodora, the stepdaughter of the Emperor Maximian, who was deemed a more suitable bride.

In the meantime, though, Helena had had a baby. Constantine was born in 272. We know very little about his early years; we know even less about what happened to Helena after her husband divorced her. The next historical episode which is captured for us is the proclamation of Constantine as Caesar. This happened on his father's death in York in the year 306. The soldiers proclaimed him as successor to Constantius and Helena most likely joined his court at this time.

The emperor's mother

Helena moved to Trier, where Constantine had his main residence, and then to Rome. At the imperial palace in Trier, on the Mosel river in south-west Germany, there are still images of her in ceiling frescoes. But best of all, her image is captured for us on coins. Constantine had these made at fifteen different mints in eight countries across the Empire. What is striking about them is the similarity of the image, whatever the origin of the coin itself. Helena presents her right profile. Her hair is braided and curled around the back of her neck. She looks suitably imperious and has the names Flavia and Augusta before her own. On the reverse of the coin is a symbol of peace, with the words *securitas reipublice*. This is Helena in her prime.

When did she become a Christian? What was

her investment in Christianity? The key year is 312, when Constantine crossed into Italy to begin his imperial reign. Life for the Christian community had deteriorated under the Emperor Diocletian, who conducted a fierce persecution of the Church from 302 to 310. When Constantine crossed the Milvian Bridge to do battle with his rival, Maxentius, on 28 October 312, a new era was set to begin. The court historian Eusebius writes an ecstatic account of the battle and of the triumphal progress. Now Eusebius is a dubious witness. He is like a newspaper reporter who says that what he writes is true. But he is not a good journalist, because he is so tied up into loyalty to Constantine that he can barely tell the truth. When you read Eusebius, you have to remember that his heart was bursting with pride. Here is his account of the Battle of Milvian Bridge:

> Constantine besought his father's god in prayer, beseeching and imploring him to tell him who he was and to stretch out his right hand to help him in his present difficulties. And while he was

thus praying with fervent entreaty, a most incredible sign appeared to him from heaven, the account of which it might have been hard to believe had it been related by any other person. But since the victorious emperor himself long afterwards declared it to the writer of this history, when he was honoured with his acquaintance and society, and confirmed his statement by an oath, who could hesitate to accredit the relation, especially since the testimony of after-time has established its truth?

He said that about noon, when the day was already beginning to decline, he saw with his own eyes the trophy of a cross of light in the heavens, above the sun, and an inscription, CONQUER BY THIS, attached to it. At this sight he himself was struck with amazement, and his whole army also, which followed him on an expedition, and witnessed the miracle.

He said, moreover, that he doubted within himself what the import of this portent could be. And while he continued to ponder and reason on its meaning, night overtook him; then in his sleep the Christ of God appeared to him with the sign which he had seen in the heavens, and commanded him to make a likeness of that sign which he had seen in the heavens, and to use it as a safeguard in all engagements with his enemies.

This incident inspired the Anglo-Saxon poet Cynewulf in his *Elene*, a verse narrative of the life of Helena. He writes in the eighth century:

And unto Caesar himself in his slumber, as he slept among his train, strong in triumph, a vision was shown. Unto him it seemed a radiant warrior came, in the image of a man, gleaming and bright of hue, more fair than he had seen early or late under the heavens. He started from his slumber and donned his helmet crested with the boar. And straightway the herald, beauteous messenger of glory, spake unto him and named him by name, and the shadow of the night vanished away.

'O Constantine, the King of Angels, Wielder of fates, Lord of hosts, bids proffer thee a compact. Be not thou adread though foreign hordes threaten terror against thee and heavy war. But look thou unto heaven, unto the Warden of glory; there shalt thou find support, the token of triumph.'

Swift was he unto the bidding of that holy angel, unbound his inmost heart and gazed on high, as the herald bade him, the faithful weaver of peace. He beheld the radiant Tree of glory above the dome of clouds, bright with gems, adorned with gold; its jewels gleamed. The shining cross was written round about with characters of radiance and light: 'In this sign shalt thou overwhelm the foe in bitter need, and stay the loathsome host.'

Then the light vanished away, together with the holy herald journeyed up on high unto the company of the pure. But the king, the Prince of men, was the blither and knew the less of sorrow in his soul by that fair vision.

Then Constantine, shelter of princes and giver of treasure to men, war-lord of legions, glorious king, bade shape a like symbol speedily, even as he beheld the beacon, revealed to him in the heavens, the cross of Christ. He bade

at break of day, at early dawn, to wake the
warriors and the weapon-storm, to raise the
battle standard and carry on before him that
holy tree, into the throng of foes to bear God's
beacon. Trumpets sang aloud before the hosts,
the ravens had joy of the work; the dewy-
feathered eagle scanned the march, the strife of
savage men; the wolf, comrade of the wood,
lifted up his howl. The terror of battle was
come.

Eusebius takes up the story:

Then he rode into Rome with songs of victory,
and together with women and tiny children, all
members of the Senate and whole populace of
Rome, turning out in force and with shining
eyes and all their heart welcomed him as deliv-
erer, saviour, and benefactor, singing his praises
with insatiate joy.

Eusebius attributes Constantine's victory to God
who had called him to fight under the banner of
the cross. The cross was set to be a banner of vic-

tory, a sign of hope to the winners and of terror and slaughter to the losers. How could it ever become more than that?

The conversion of Constantine

The following year, Constantine and his fellow emperor, Licinius who ruled in the east, issued a decree of religious tolerance. The Edict of Milan granted freedom to Christians. Just before his own death in 337, Constantine himself would be baptised, delaying this event until the last possible moment, to ensure eternal salvation for himself. Despite all the accolades of Eusebius, his reign would at times be a brutal one: he executed his own father-in-law, three brothers-in-law, Fausta his wife and Crispus his son, Helena's grandchild.

As the experience of persecution and suffering faded for the Christian community, so the Church moved into the light. One of the most visual ways it did this was by beginning to build magnificent basilicas and to adorn these with works of art. In the early Church, even in the catacombs where they originally worshipped, artists had preferred to depict Jesus as the Good Shepherd, a benign image of the Saviour. Alternatively he was shown exercising power, casting out demons, raising Lazarus from the dead or surrounded by his apostles in triumph. When the first basilicas were built, the curved apse at the head of the nave provided a dramatic backdrop for further scenes of glory. Christ sits in glory, clad for all the world like Constantine – that is with a tunic and pallium, holding a book in his left hand, his right hand raised in blessing.

How could the cross, the sign by which Constantine conquered, be reclaimed in this heady, triumphant world? How could the image of redemption be reinvented?

The search for the true cross

From 393 to 396, a woman called Egeria went on pilgrimage, touring through Egypt, Palestine, Edessa, Asia Minor and Constantinople, the city which Constantine made his capital on assuming control of the whole Empire in 324. She wrote a diary as she travelled and so provides us with an early eye-witness account of the architectural splendours she saw, as well as of the religious ceremonies she attended. Of Jerusalem, she wrote:

> Since it is Sunday, at dawn they assemble for the liturgy in the major church built by Constantine and located on Golgotha behind the Cross ... After the people have rested, everyone gathers together again in the major church on Golgotha at the beginning of the second hour. It would be superfluous to describe how the churches – the Anastasis, the Cross, and the church in Bethlehem – are decorated on that day. You see nothing there but gold and gems and silk. If you look at the hangings, they are made of silk with gold stripes; if you look at the curtains, they are also made of silk with gold stripes. Every kind of sacred vessel brought out on that day is of gold inlaid with precious stones. How could the weight and number of the candle holders, the candelabra, the lamps, and of the various sacred vessels be in any way estimated and noted down? And what can I say about the decoration of this

building which Constantine, with his mother on hand, had embellished with as much gold, mosaics, and marble as the resources of his empire permitted – and not only the major church, but the Anastasis as well, and the Cross and the other holy places in Jerusalem?

Would that Helena herself had kept a journal of comparable interest. For she too had visited Jerusalem and the other eastern provinces of the Empire in 327. She was a woman of nearly eighty at the time. Eusebius takes up the story:

Having resolved to discharge the duties of pious devotion to the God, the king of kings, and feeling it incumbent on her to render thanks-givings with prayers on behalf both of her son, now so mighty an emperor, and of his sons, her own grandchildren, the divinely favoured Caesars, though now advanced in years, yet gifted with no common degree of wisdom, she had hastened with youthful alacrity to survey this venerable land; and at the same time to visit the eastern provinces, cities, and peoples with a truly imperial solicitude. As soon, then, as she had rendered due reverence to the ground which the Saviour's feet had trodden, according to the prophetic word which says, 'Let us worship at the place whereon his feet have stood,' she immediately bequeathed the fruit of her piety to future generations.

For without delay she dedicated two churches to the God whom she adored, one at the grotto which had been the scene of the Saviour's birth; the other on the mount of his ascension.

This latter church consisted of a complex of buildings. The Anastasis was a round church, on the site of Christ's burial tomb, known as the Holy Sepulchre. There was also a Calvary, an open-air building on the site of the crucifixion. And finally there was a Martyrium, an oblong basilica on the site where the true cross was discovered.

For in Jerusalem, Helena had a further purpose. She was more than a casual pilgrim or even a dedicated builder of churches. She was determined to find the cross on which Jesus died. She herself was to die the following year, and her extreme old age gave her an added incentive for her quest. It took her to the site of Golgotha. It took her into an underground cavern. Later generations would have a two-fold reason for gratitude to Helena. She is alleged to have found the true cross and so to have given her world an important icon which would help people venerate God. But more importantly she opened a floodgate. For theology could now become more rounded, with the restoration of the sense of glory in weakness which had inspired the Apostle Paul: 'We proclaim Christ crucified, a stumbling block to Jews and foolishness to Gentiles, but to those who are the called, both Jews and Greeks, Christ the power of God and the wisdom of God. For God's foolishness is wiser than human wisdom, and God's weakness is stronger than human strength.' (1 Corinthians 1.23)

In the 340s, the great bishop of Jerusalem, Cyril, gave a series of sermons. He is the first to mention this discovery and to consider its theological implications. He writes with a new voice for a new age:

> He was truly crucified for our sins. For if you would deny it, this place visibly refutes you, this blessed Golgotha, in which we are now assembled for the sake of him who was here crucified; and the whole world has since been filled with pieces of the wood of the cross. But he was crucified not for sins of his own, but that we might be delivered from our sins. And though as man he was at that time despised of men and was buffeted, yet he was acknowledged by the Creation as God; for when the sun saw his Lord dishonoured, he grew dim and trembled, not enduring the sight. (Catecheses 4.10)

> The holy wood of the cross bears witness, seen among us to this day, and from this place now almost filling the whole world by means of those who, in faith, take portions from it. (Catecheses 10.19)

> Jesus really suffered for all, for the cross was no illusion, otherwise our redemption is an illusion also. His death was not a mere show, for then is our salvation also fabulous. His Passion

then was real: for he was really crucified, and we are not ashamed thereat; he was crucified and we deny it not, nay, I rather glory to speak of it. For though I should now deny it, here is Golgotha to confute me, near which we are now assembled; the wood of the cross confutes me, which was afterwards distributed piecemeal from hence to all the world. I confess the cross because I know the Resurrection. (Catecheses 13.4)

With the discovery of the true cross, the words glory and shame, humiliation and truth, honour and resurrection get reinvented. That is why the story of Helena is a myth for us to ponder, rather than a legend – albeit a pious one – which we should dismiss.

PART TWO

The Wisdom of Helena

'I confess the Cross
because I know the Resurrection'

PART TWO

—◆—

'I confess the Cross because I know the Resurrection'

When Helena died, Eusebius wrote,

When at length at the close of a long life, she was called to inherit a happier lot, having arrived at the eightieth year of her age, and being very near the time of her departure, she prepared and executed her last will. Having thus made her will, this thrice blessed woman died in the presence of her illustrious son, who was in attendance at her side, caring for her and held her hands: so that, to those who rightly discerned the truth, the thrice blessed one seemed not to die, but to experience a real change and transition from an earthly to a heavenly existence, since her soul, remoulded as it were into an incorruptible and angelic essence, was received up into her Saviour's presence.

Her body too, was honoured with special tokens of respect, being escorted on its way to the imperial city by a vast train of guards, and there deposited in a royal tomb. Such were the last days of the emperor's mother, a person worthy of being had in perpetual remembrance, both for her own practical piety, and because she had given birth to so extraordinary and admirable an offspring.'

She was buried in Rome in the mausoleum near the Church of Saints Marcellino and Pietro on the Via Labicana. Her remains are preserved in a porphyry sarcophagus which lies in the Vatican Museum. Much is buried along with her remains, yet her story survived in historical texts, and it survives in our imagination too.

Understanding Helena's story
So how are we to understand Helena's story? Is it a legend, with embellishments from Eusebius? After all, his desire to show Constantine in a good light on every occasion makes him a dubious witness. Even the death-bed narrative

has the cameras fully trained on Constantine, while Helena features as the mother of a great son, who holds her hands tenderly as she dies. She prefigures Monica, the mother of Augustine and all the other mothers of great sons who have had a walk-on part in the life story of their august progeny. Was her association with the true cross a simple fiction? Was it a pious fabrication, designed to enhance the reputation of the age of Constantine, or what? What does it mean to venerate the cross, to set up a dialogue with the cross, to hold up an instrument of torture as an image of glory?

The myth of Helena's story only works if these questions are addressed. According to this myth, she sought the true cross, not some fictive or phoney cross. If we ask what it means to seek a true cross, then some of the other questions get answered on the way.

True and false crosses
There is enough documentary evidence – however biased the people who wrote it – to piece together a coherent account of Helena's life.

There is enough devotional evidence to show that the discovery of the cross meant a great deal to Christianity as it emerged from persecution and became accepted in the Roman Empire. What is curious is that a suffering community sought for glory and for interpretations of the life and ministry of Jesus that put great emphasis on his power, whereas an imperially-sanctioned Church turned to the cross for meaning. While it was struggling for acceptance, Christianity could not afford to look at the mystery of Jesus' stripping and death as a common criminal. Once it had achieved acceptance, it could rediscover the mystery of strength in weakness.

Taking up the true cross
Is it the case that we can only handle our own weakness from a position of strength? One of the hardest lines in the gospel is a piece of Jesus' teaching which examines this idea. 'He called the crowd with his disciples, and said to them, "If any want to become my followers, let them deny themselves and take up their cross and follow me. For those who want to save their life will

lose it, and those who lose their life for my sake, and for the sake of the gospel, will save it"' (Mark 8.34–5). Jesus calls for selflessness. He takes it for granted that each of us has a burden to shoulder, and suggests that true selflessness will only be achieved by those who embrace their burden or cross.

This could sound like depressing news were it not for the sentence which begins, 'If any want to become my followers ...' He promises a relationship to those who are prepared to take this step. They will experience a sense of their need for God, and they will follow Jesus. A call to selflessness heard in total isolation would be an abusive call, were it not hemmed in by the assurance of these promises.

The Church has not always understood this. A true cross is one which is embraced freely and with love. People will seek it out with all the determination of a Helena if it speaks accurately to their condition, if it is their cross. A false cross is one which someone else invents and imposes as an alien discipline. There are powerful examples of this from history. For centuries the

Church sanctioned slavery, or religious discrimination and persecution – the Crusades make a telling example of this; for centuries, certain groups have been disenfranchised by the Church – women, for instance, have been punished by being told that they are inferior to men; for centuries, a sick asceticism punished the body, in the name of a doctrine which exalted the soul. False crosses – even those which are mistakenly imposed by the Church – must be resisted at all costs, for they crush the human spirit.

This tendency to persecute other people erupts in our own personal lives too. In our relationships we invent crosses or burdens for each other. We have unrealistic expectations; we hope for too much; we make each other in our own image and likeness, rather than accepting each other as made in God's image and likeness. We crucify each other in the name of our prejudices and our own choices, let alone our values and beliefs.

The most tortuous crosses of all are those we impose upon ourselves. Self-hatred is destructive. It is unremitting in that it does not go away. We write scripts within our own heads and use these to persecute ourselves. They begin, 'If only …', and they are terribly unforgiving. They begin, 'Of course …', and they have a destructive inner logic from which there is no escape. They begin, 'There is no hope …' and lead us to depression or to flirt with death.

Where does true freedom lie? The quest of the emperor's mother becomes an important myth for understanding these patterns. Flavia Augusta Helena, the woman whose image was carried on coins from one end of the Empire to the other, who was attended wherever she went, who enjoyed power and authority, this Helena went to look for the true cross. She sought understanding in a source outside of herself. She did not simply chew over her own experience and marvel at the forces which brought her from her humble origins, through marriage to an ambitious soldier, the wilderness years of her divorce and abandonment and then to the heady exultation of Constantine's rise to power. She did more than this. She knew that something was missing, and went out to look for it.

With her imperial status, she was able to make a new journey and a new discovery. A true cross can best be chosen by someone who knows about power and authority. The truly selfless, those who take up their cross daily, are people who have a good enough sense of self to be able to let go of it, to give it away. A doctrine of the true cross never sanctions cruelty or oppression. It calls us all to glory and then to freedom. This sense of glory is hard to describe, because it appears to go against the humility of the gospel. But it is there in the gospel text. From the moment the angel appears to Mary, we know that she is called to glory. From the moment she embraces her cousin Elizabeth, this sense of glory and purpose has a theme tune. The *Magnificat* tells out Mary's soul; it focuses on the greatness and the glory of the Lord, but is sung in the conviction that God reverses the assumptions by which we live. The lonely and the humble and the sad and the depressed will be exalted. People who believe in their own self-importance will be deflated.

The pain of unbidden crosses

But what about the crosses and burdens we do not choose? How do they work? Helena's story is a powerful reminder of the sheer burden of human living. We make choices which prove to be more costly than we anticipated. Our best laid plans collapse. The energy of youth gives way to the wisdom of experience, but not in a straight line, a direct trajectory. Growing up hurts. The edges are knocked off us, and a whole lot more besides. The temptation is to think that there is some kind of malice in all of this, that someone is out to get us. The truth is rather more stark than this.

The doctrine of original sin had not been fully elaborated by the Church of Helena's conversion. It would only be fully formulated later. But the fact of original sin was plain for her to see. That is why Cyril of Jerusalem could preach so tellingly about the resurrection. A society which does not believe in sin is unable to acknowledge its need for redemption. Words like salvation and grace and heaven begin to sound disembodied or meaningless. They have no bite.

So Cyril is speaking to us now, as well as to his own world. As he saw it, the resurrection gives us the certainty that we are freed from sin by an incarnate Redeemer. The resurrection tells us that Jesus is our Saviour. But without the cross there would be no salvation. It stands as a great linch-pin in our understanding, linking the certainty that Jesus was born, that he had a human body, that he really was incarnate, with the certainty that he rose again after death. The cross confirms the public death of Jesus.

So we look at the cross through the prism of the incarnation and the resurrection. None of the Christian mysteries can be separated out to the exclusion of the others. A crucified saviour is a risen and ascended saviour. The cross and glory belong together. The instrument of shame and horror becomes the sign of redemption. This does not get rid of human fallibility at a stroke, but it does offer a way through. It offers a theol-ogy for understanding human crassness and for disclosing the generosity of God in securing our salvation. Helena's world, like our own, needed just such a theology.

The consolation of the cross

The Good Friday liturgy in any Christian church can be a bleak and horrible affair if it has no solemnity about it. Genuine liturgical reverence and solemnity guide us to the truth. For when we approach the cross we do something incredibly important. An empress led us there, just as she was led with her retinue and her hangers-on to make her way to Jerusalem. The myth of Helena speaks eloquently to our sense of what it is to venerate the cross. To understand this, we need to examine our attitude towards relics. Are they simply memorabilia, like the contents of a well-loved home? Are they faintly disgusting – old bones and old wood which should be buried and forgotten? Do they make people superstitious because they act like religious fetishes?

St Jerome wrote, 'We do not worship, we do not adore, for fear that we should bow down to the creature rather than to the Creator, but we venerate the relics of the martyrs in order the better to adore Him whose martyrs they are.' This, in a nutshell, is the orthodox explanation of what it means to hold relics in some kind of religious esteem. They lead us to God.

So how, in particular, does the cross lead us to God? It calls us to selflessness as we have seen. It enables us to hand ourselves over to God. But it does more than that. It enables us to perform rituals that are just as significant as Helena's long pilgrimage to Jerusalem. The cross 'works' on a symbolic level as well as a practical one. It is the primary symbol of the sufferings of Jesus, as well as the image of all our burdens.

Good Friday liturgies and comparable rituals have a long history. The devotional exercise known as the Stations of the Cross takes us down the same liturgical route. The fourteen stations or stops along the route have all the hallmarks of good liturgy. We follow the events that took Jesus from his judgment by Pontius Pilate, through the humiliation of his scourging and crowning with thorns, to the place of crucifixion. We stay with him while he dies and when his body is taken down from cross, we see his mother receive it 'with unutterable tenderness'. This is the gospel narrative set out as in a

Mystery Play, actually re-enacted in front of our eyes. And, as in a Mystery Play, we watch the other characters, Mary his mother, Simon of Cyrene who helps him carry the cross, Veronica who wipes his face with a cloth, the soldiers who gamble and cast lots for his seamless garment. We are invited to position ourselves in this cast of characters, to take up our station or stand as Jesus goes to his death on a cross. This is the exact opposite of a triumphal march. Jesus falls repeatedly, as we all do. At the end he is taken to the blessed cold of a new tomb and laid to rest. We walk away from the experience with new understanding of the cost and burden of love.

This is the intention of rituals which surround the veneration of the cross. By inviting us to reflect on the sufferings of Jesus, they are not doing something macabre. They are calling us into a new relationship with our wounded saviour.

This insight is captured in the fourteenth-century hymn 'Soul of my saviour':

Soul of my saviour,
    sanctify my breast;
Body of Christ,
    be thou my saving guest;
Blood of my saviour,
    bathe me in thy tide,
wash me with water,
    flowing from thy side.

Strength and protection
    may thy Passion be;
O Blessed Jesus
    hear and answer me;
deep in thy wounds, Lord,
    hide and shelter me;
so shall I never,
    never part from thee.

Guard and defend me
    from the foe malign;
in death's dread moments
    make me only thine;
call me, and bid me
    come to thee on high,
when I may praise thee
    with thy saints for aye.

The truest of crosses

Death is the final burden. Death is our great fear. A true devotion to the cross of Jesus removes some of the sting of that fear. For the truest of crosses, the one on which Jesus died, is the sign of our redemption. At the foot of the cross we are all judged. As Paul wrote to the Romans, 'There is no distinction, since all have sinned and fall short of the glory of God; they are now justified by his grace as a gift, through the redemption that is in Christ Jesus, whom God put forward as a sacrifice of atonement by his blood, effective through faith (Romans 3.23–5). And at the foot of the cross we are all redeemed through faith.

Helena died on her return from Jerusalem. She was now safe in the knowledge that Jesus had died for her, and that her redemption was complete. In the *Victimae Paschali laudes* or Easter Sequence, the Church would later sing out the truth of this mystery:

Christians, to the Paschal Victim offer sacrifice
and praise.
The sheep are ransomed by the Lamb;
and Christ, the undefiled,
hath sinners to his Father reconciled.
Death with life contending: combat strangely
ended!
Life's own Champion, slain, yet lives to reign.
Tell us, Mary: say what thou didst see upon the
way.
The tomb the Living did enclose;
I saw Christ's glory as he rose!
The angels were attesting;
shroud with grave-clothes resting.
Christ, my hope, has risen: he goes before you
into Galilee.
That Christ is truly risen from the dead we
know.
Victorious King, thy mercy show!
Amen.

The place of memory

The community which Helena joined when she became a Christian was a worshipping community. At the centre of its worship was the celebration of the Eucharist, an act of re-membering and of thanksgiving to God. What was remembered was the passion and sacrificial death of Jesus and the final meal that he ate with his friends. A eucharistic community is one which gives thanks for the work of Jesus on the cross.

Why does the memory of the cross remain so important to Christianity? Is there something rather gruesome about this obsession or can it speak to our own spiritual quest? One answer to this question comes when the story of the cross is read alongside the account of the Last Supper. At his final meal with his friends Jesus himself did two things which we still call to mind when celebrating the Eucharist.

First, according to John's gospel, he wrapped a towel around his waist, knelt on the ground in front of his apostles, and washed their feet. He changed the role of host for that of a servant, reversing their expectations, reminding them that the Messiah was to be an ambivalent figure. Isaiah had written of the sufferings which would be borne by the one who was to come:

Who has believed what we have heard? And to whom has the arm of the Lord been revealed? For he grew up before him like a young plant, and like a root out of dry ground; he had no form or majesty that we should look at him, nothing in his appearance that we should desire him. He was despised and rejected by others; a man of suffering and acquainted with infirmity; and as one from whom others hide their faces he was despised, and we held him of no account. Surely he has borne our infirmities and carried our diseases; yet we accounted him stricken, struck down by God, and afflicted. But he was wounded for our transgressions, crushed for our iniquities; upon him was the punishment that made us whole, and by his bruises we are healed. All we like sheep have gone astray; we have all turned to our own way, and the Lord has laid on him the iniquity of us all. He was oppressed, and he was afflicted, yet he did not open his mouth; like a lamb that is led to the slaughter, and like a sheep that before its shearers is silent, so he did not open his mouth. By a perversion of justice he was taken away. Who could have imagined his future? For he was cut off from the land of the living, stricken for the transgression of my people. (Isaiah 53.1–8)

Whether we like it or not – and the Early Church did not like it – Jesus was treated as a common criminal. His crucifixion was the punishment for felony as well as for our sins. When he washed the feet of his friends, he signalled his new identity to them. He was to become their inferior and he was to make them clean.

The other gospel writers tell us of about the meal itself. This was a solemn, ritual meal. During it Jesus took bread, blessed, broke and gave it to his friends. This is Mark's account:

While they were eating, he took a loaf of bread, and after blessing it he broke it, gave it to them, and said, 'Take; this is my body.' Then he took a cup, and after giving thanks he gave it to them, and all of them drank from it. He said to them, 'This is my blood of the covenant, which is poured out for many. Truly I tell you, I will never again drink of the fruit of the vine until that day when I drink it new in the kingdom of God.' When they had sung the hymn, they went out to the Mount of Olives. (Mark 14.22–6)

Jesus took, blessed, broke and gave. On the cross he was taken, blessed, broken and given for the salvation of the world. What does this mean? The order of these actions is important. To be taken is to be selected, chosen, identified as desirable. To be chosen by God is to enter into a relationship which binds us into being: 'For I am convinced that neither death, nor life, nor angels, nor rulers, nor things present, nor things to come, nor powers, nor height, nor depth, nor anything else in all creation, will be able to separate us from the love of God in Christ Jesus our Lord.' (Romans 8.38–9)

In the Old Testament God chose judges and prophets and kings, people whose task was to serve the people by good governance. In the New Testament, Jesus chooses the poor and the needy, the rich young man, the Pharisee named Nicodemus who was a leader of the Jews. He chooses named women and named men to serve and to follow him. This choice implies desire, love, a sense of election and of self-worth. Jesus himself is chosen as well. God chooses him from all eternity. The crowds seek him out, they pursue him, demanding more miracles, more teaching, more meetings, more healings. The pattern is one of intense desire.

The Christian spiritual tradition uses the language of desire shamelessly when talking about the relationship we enjoy with God. This piece was written by a medieval mystic, Marguerite d'Oingt:

> For are you not my mother and more than my mother? The mother who bore me laboured in delivering me for one day and one night but you, my sweet and lovely Lord, laboured for me for more than thirty years. Ah, with what love you laboured for me and bore me through your

whole life. But when the time approached for you to be delivered, your labour pains were so great that your holy sweat was like great drops of blood that came out from your body and fell on the earth. When the hour of your delivery came you were placed on the hard bed of the cross and your nerves and all your veins burst when in one day you gave birth to the whole world.

In our own relationships we know about this desire: we call it falling in love. We know about it in our work and hobbies too, in whatever moves us to self-gift. For the sense of being chosen leads us to offer ourselves in love where we are chosen and known in love.

That is why we need to be blessed before the gift of self is accepted by God. Jesus blesses the bread, gives thanks to God for it. He too is blessed and so can go safely to the place where all will be taken from him as he is stripped and offered to God for our salvation. Only those who are blessed, those for whom we give thanks to God, can fulfil a religious purpose in our lives.

That is why we need saints such as Helena, people who are clearly blessed by God, people who can remind us of our own blessedness.

The blessed, those who know that they are the beloved of God, may safely go with Jesus to the place of self-offering and self-gift: to the cross. When Jesus took bread at the Last Supper, when he blessed it, he also broke it. For without the breaking, there can be no gift. There can be no sharing. This ultimately is the meaning of the great action of Jesus upon the cross. For here he is taken, blessed, broken and given for the salvation of the world. Where once he was known and loved by particular friends in particular circumstances, he is now raised up, exalted and given for all.

Devotion to the cross of Jesus
When we venerate the cross of Jesus, we embrace a spirituality which forces us to go on a journey. We have to move beyond the horror and shame of a criminal's death; we have to move beyond sentimental piety; we have to look on the face of 'one from whom others hide their faces' for 'he

was despised, and they held him of no account'.

With Helena we go to Jerusalem, we go to the place of suffering in the conviction that our life will be incomplete without this journey. We go in the conviction that this will be a hard journey, that we cannot know its outcome, for we may not discover a true cross. We may not understand the full extent of our own suffering, we may not experience the depth of the knowledge of God's love revealed to us in the suffering of Jesus. We may not even be relieved of our own guilt.

Nevertheless we make the journey and Helena can inspire us as we travel. The myth of the Mother and Empress who went before us reminds us that this is a royal task, and so that it is part of our destiny and part of our dignity that we venture to understand the sufferings of Jesus and so to understand our own.

When Helena died there were two images of her left for posterity. The mother of Constantine is commemorated on two coins. The first shows her with her hair braided around her neck, as a young woman intent on conquering the world. The other shows the mature Helena with her hair tied up. This second coin is larger and more splendid. It is a testimony to the wisdom that she gained as she travelled to the outer edges of her experience and came back with a message for us all.

PART THREE

Prayers And Writings

PART THREE

Prayers and Readings

The Christian community has always struggled to have a proper balance in its devotional life and to understand the place of the cross within spirituality. Here are readings and prayers which illustrate parts of this journey into wisdom.

Justin Martyr
1st century

For consider all the things in the world, whether without this form they could be administered or have any community. For the sea is not traversed except that trophy, which is called a sail, abide safe in the ship; and the earth is not ploughed without it: diggers and mechanics do not their work, except with tools which have this shape.

59

And the human form differs from that of the irrational animals in nothing else than in its being erect and having the hands extended, and having on the face extending from the forehead what is called the nose, through which there is respiration for the living creature; and this shows no other form than that of the cross.

The Word of the Cross: Paulinus of Nola
4th century

Look on the God, Christ hidden in our flesh.
A bitter word, the cross, and bitter sight:
Yet sweet it is; for God upon that tree
Did offer up His life: upon that rood
My Life hung, that my life might stand in God.
Christ, what am I to give Thee for my life?
Unless I take from Thy hands the cup they hold.

To cleanse me with the precious draught of
    death.
What shall I do? My body to be burned?
Make myself vile? The debt's not paid out yet.
Whate'er I do, it is but I and Thou,
And still do I come short, still must Thou pay
My debts, O Christ; for debts Thyself hadst
    none.
What love may balance Thine? My Lord was
    found
In fashion like a slave, that so His slave
Might find himself in fashion like his Lord.

Think you the bargain's hard, to have exchanged
The transient for the eternal, to have sold
Earth to buy heaven? More dearly God bought
   me.

The Dream of the Rood: Cynewulf
9th century

Listen, I want to tell the best of dreams,
that came to me in a vision in the middle of the
    night,
when other people were in bed.
It seemed to me that I saw the best tree,
lifted into the air surrounded by light,
the brightest of trees. The whole symbol was
covered with gold; beautiful jewels stood
at the surface of the earth, and also five were
on the crossbeam.
All those fair by eternal decree gazed at
the angel of the Lord there;
certainly it was not the cross of a criminal,
but holy spirits watched on it there,
and men and women watched over the earth
and all this glorious creation.

The tree of victory was rare, and I was guilty of
    sins,
and sorely wounded with sins.
I saw the tree of glory

adorned with clothes shining beautifully,
covered with gold; jewels had
covered splendidly the Lord's tree.
However, I could perceive through that gold
ancient hostility of wretched ones, that it first
     began
to bleed on the right side.
I was completely disturbed with sorrows;
I was afraid of that wonderful sight
I saw that eager symbol changing clothing and
     colour :
sometimes it was drenched with blood,
soaked with streams of blood,
sometimes it was decorated with treasure.
However, I, laying there for a long time,
sorrowful beheld the tree of the Saviour,
until I heard it made a noise;
then the best wood began to speak words :

'It was years ago – yet I remember it –
that I was cut down at the end of a forest,
removed from my root. Strong enemies took me
     there,
and made me a spectacle for themselves there,

64

and they made me raise up their criminals;
the warriors carried me on their shoulders,
until they set me upon a hill;
many enemies fastened me there.
I saw the Lord of all
hurry with great zeal, in his wish to ascend on
  me.
There I did not dare to bow or burst
against the word of the Lord, when I saw
the surface of the earth tremble. I was able
to fell all enemies, but I stood fast.
The young warrior undressed himself – that was
  God almighty! –
strong and resolute; he climbed the high cross,
brave in the sight of many, because he wanted to
  redeem us.
I trembled when the warrior embraced me;
however, I did not dare to bow to the earth,
to fall to the surfaces of the earth, but I had to
  stand firmly.
I was raised up as the cross, I raised up the great
  King,
Lord of heavens, I did not dare to bend myself.

They pierced me with dark nails; the wounds are
    visible on me,
open malicious wounds; I did not dare to injure
    any of them.
They insulted us both together, I was completely
    drenched with blood, poured from the man's
    side, after he had sent his spirit.

'I experienced on the hill many
awful events : I saw the God of hosts
cruelly stretched out. Darkness had
covered the body of the Lord with clouds,
bright light; shadow went forth,
darkness under the clouds. All that was alive
    wept,
with the fall of the King : Christ was on the
    cross.
However, hastening ones came there from afar
to the Prince; I saw it all.
Sorely I was troubled with sorrows, however I
    bent down to the man's hand
humble, with great zeal. They took the almighty
    God,
and they lifted him from the heavy punishment;

the warriors left me standing drenched with blood;

I was all wounded by arrows.

They laid down the weary body there; they stood at the head of his body;

they saw the Lord of heaven there, and he rested there for a while,

tired after the great struggle.

Then the men began to make a tomb for him in the sight of the slayer,

they carved it of bright stone;

they set the Lord of victory herein.

They began to sing a lament for him

sorrowed in the evening, then they wanted to travel back,

tired from the famous Prince.

He rested there with little company.

However, we stood there crying for a long time

on our foundation; the voice of the soldiers

went up; the body cooled down,

beautiful body. The men began to fell us all down

to the earth; that was a terrible event!

The men buried us in a deep ditch;

however, there the Disciples of the Lord,
the friends found out,
and adorned me with gold and silver.

'Now you could hear, my beloved man,
that I have experienced the work of evildoers,
from sore sorrows. Now the time has come
that, far and wide, honour me
men on earth and all the wonderful creation,
pray themselves to this symbol. On me the Son
    of God
suffered a while; therefore I rise up now
gloriously under the heavens, and I can save
everyone of those in whom there is fear of me.
Formerly I had become the hardest of
    punishment,
most hateful to people, before I opened for them
the right way of life then, for the men.
Listen, the Prince of glory, the Guardian of the
    heaven,
honoured me over the trees in the forest,
just as the almighty God also honoured his
    mother, Mary herself,
before all men, over all women's kin.

'Now I call you, my dear man,
that you tell this vision to others;
reveal with words that it is the cross of glory,
that the almighty Lord suffered on
for your many sins
and the former actions of Adam.
There he tasted death; but the Lord rose again
with his great power to help all.
Then he rose to the heavens. From there he will
    set out again
to this world to seek humankind
on Doomsday the Lord himself,
the almighty Lord and with his angels,
in that He, who has the power of judgment, will
    judge
each one, according to how he earned for
    himself earlier
here in this temporary life.
No one there can be unafraid
of the word that the Lord says :
he will ask publicly where the man is,
he who for the name of God would be willing to
    taste
the bitter death, as he did before on the cross.

And then they begin to fear and think little
what they say to Christ.
Then there no one dares to be terrified
who before bore him, the best of symbols, in his
    breast.

Celtic Devotion

I know that I hung
on a wind-rocked tree
nine whole nights
with spear wounded
myself to myself
on that tree
on which no-one knows
from which root it springs.

None gave me bread
none gave me drink
down to the depths I peered
to snatch up runes
with a roaring screech
and fall in a dizzied faint.

Well-being I won
and wisdom too
I grew and joyed in my growth
from a word to a word
I was led to a word
from a deed to another deed.

Prayer to the Holy Cross: St Anselm
11th century

Holy Cross, which calls to mind the cross
 whereon our Lord Jesus Christ died,
to bring us back from that eternal death to which
 our misery was leading us, to the eternal life
 we had lost by sinning.
I adore, I venerate, and I glory in that cross
 which you represent to us, and by that cross I
 adore our merciful Lord and what he has in
 mercy done for us.
Cross, worthy to be loved, in whom is our
 salvation, our life, and resurrection.
Most precious wood, by whom we are saved and
 set free,
sign to be reverenced, by which we are sealed for
 God, glorious cross, we ought to glory only
 in you.

We do not acknowledge you because of the
 cruelty that godless and foolish men prepared
 you to effect upon the most gentle Lord, but
 because of the wisdom and goodness of him

who of his own free will took you up. For
they could not have done anything unless his
wisdom had permitted it,

and he could not suffer except that in his mercy
he willed it.

They chose you

that they might carry out their evil deeds;

he chose you

that he might fulfil the work of his goodness.

They that by you

they might hand over the righteous to death;

he that through you he might save sinners from
death.

They that they might kill life;

he that he might destroy death.

They that they might condemn the Saviour;

he that he might save the condemned.

They that they might bring death to the living;

he to bring life to the dead.

They acted foolishly and cruelly; he wisely and
mercifully.

Therefore, O Cross to be wondered at,

we do not value you because of the intention of
their cruel folly,

but according to the working of mercy and
    wisdom.

In what way, then, shall I praise you,
how shall I exalt you,
with what love shall I pray to you,
and with what joy shall I glory in you?
By you hell is despoiled,
by you its mouth is stopped up to all the
    redeemed.
By you demons are made afraid and restrained,
conquered and trampled underfoot.
By you the world is renewed and made beautiful
    with truth,
governed by the light of righteousness.
By you sinful humanity is justified,
the condemned are saved,
the servants of sin and hell are set free,
the dead are raised to life.
By you the blessed city in heaven
is restored and made perfect.
By you God, the Son of God, willed for our
    sakes
'to become obedient to the Father, even unto
death',

because of which he is exalted and has received
'the name which is above every name'.
By you 'his throne is prepared' and his kingdom
established.

O Cross, chosen and prepared for such ineffable
good,
the work that was accomplished on you exalts
you more than all the praises of human or
angelic thought and tongue. In you and
through you is my life and my salvation; in
you and through you is the whole and all my
good;
'forbid that I should glory save in you'.
For why was I conceived and born, and given
life, if afterwards I am to descend to hell?
If that is to be my fate it were better for me if I
had never been conceived.
And it is certain that it would have been so if I
had not been redeemed by you.

With what love shall I glory in you, O Cross,
when without you there would be nothing
for me to glory in, and in eternity I should
have the grief and misery of hell? With what

delight will I rejoice in you, when by you the servitude of hell which I inherited is exchanged for the kingdom of heaven? With what jubilation shall I laud you, when without you I faced that future which horrifies me, even if it had lasted only a moment, and through you I now expect to rejoice in eternity? Though now I serve God between hope and fear, I am sure that if I give thanks, love, and live to your glory, through you I shall at last come to that good.

So let my glory be through you and in you;
let my true hope be through you and in you.
By you my sins are wiped out,
by you my soul is dead to its old life
and lives to the new life of righteousness.
I beseech you, wash me by baptism from the sins
in which I was conceived and born,
and cleanse me again from those that I committed
after I was reborn,
so that by you I may come to those good things
for which we were created,
by the might of the same Jesus Christ our Lord
who is blessed for ever and ever. Amen.

Anon: collection of Joshua Smith, New Hampshire, 1784

The tree of life my soul hath seen,
Laden with fruit, and always green:
The trees of nature fruitless be
Compared with Christ the apple tree.

His beauty doth all things excel:
By faith I know, but ne'er can tell
The glory which I now can see
in Jesus Christ the apple tree.

For happiness I long have sought,
And pleasure dearly I have bought:
I missed of all; but now I see
'Tis found in Christ the apple tree.

I'm weary with my former toil,
Here I will sit and rest awhile:
Under the shadow I will be,
Of Jesus Christ the apple tree.

This fruit doth make my soul to thrive,
It keeps my dying faith alive;
Which makes my soul in haste to be
With Jesus Christ the apple tree.

Hymn to the Cross: Elizabeth Cecilia Clephane
19th century

Beneath the cross of Jesus
I fain would take my stand –
The shadow of a mighty rock
Within a weary land;
A home within a wilderness,
A rest upon the way,
From the burning of the noontide heat
And the burden of the day.

O safe and happy shelter,
O refuge tried and sweet,
O trysting-place where heaven's love
And heaven's justice meet!
As to the holy patriarch
That wondrous dream was given,
So seems my Saviour's cross to me
A ladder up to heaven.

I take, O cross, thy shadow,
For my abiding-place!

I ask no other sunshine than
The sunshine of his face;
Content to let the world go by,
To know no gain or loss –
My sinful self my only shame,
My glory all - the cross.

FURTHER READING

FURTHER READING

Brown, Peter, *The World of Late Antiquity,* Thames and Hudson, 1991.

Chadwick, Henry, *The Early Church,* Penguin, 1967.

Eusebius, *The History of the Church,* Penguin, 1965.

Kelly, J. N. D., *Early Christian Doctrines,* Adam and Charles Black, 1958.

Stevenson, J., *A New Eusebius,* SPCK, 1957.

Waugh, Evelyn, *Helena,* Penguin, 1963.